Christmas Songs
FOR VIBRAPHONE

ISBN 978-1-4950-2951-6

HAL•LEONARD®
CORPORATION
7777 W. BLUEMOUND RD. P.O. BOX 13819 MILWAUKEE, WI 53213

Visit Hal Leonard Online at
www.halleonard.com

Contents

Blue Christmas

Words and Music by Billy Hayes
and Jay Johnson

Do You Hear What I Hear

Words and Music by Noel Regney
and Gloria Shayne

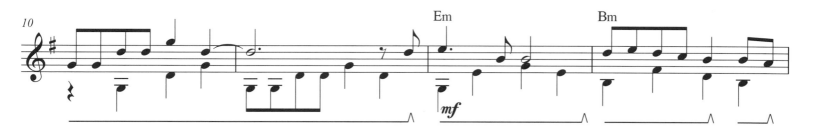

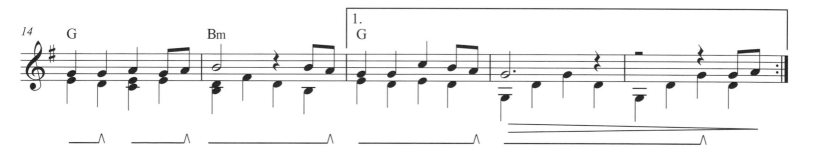

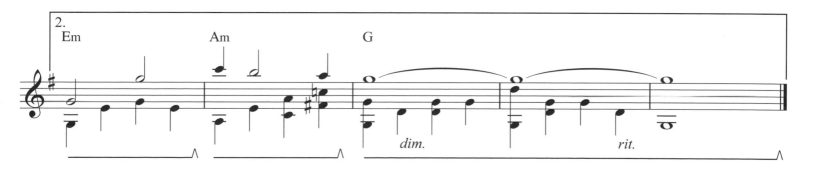

The Christmas Song
(Chestnuts Roasting on an Open Fire)

Music and Lyric by Mel Tormé
and Robert Wells

Christmas Time Is Here

Words by Lee Mendelson
Music by Vince Guaraldi

× = Mallet dampen

Frosty the Snow Man

Words and Music by Steve Nelson
and Jack Rollins

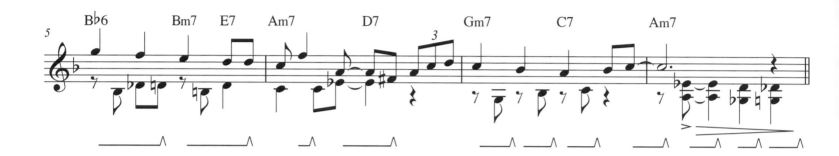

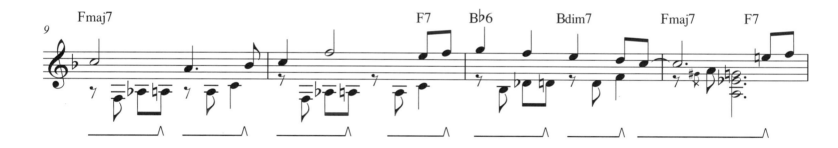

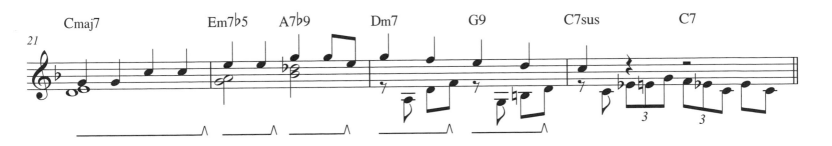

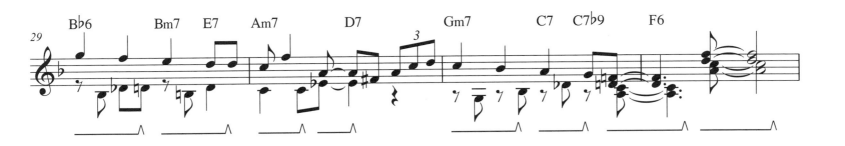

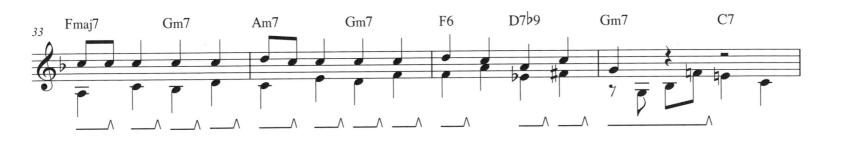

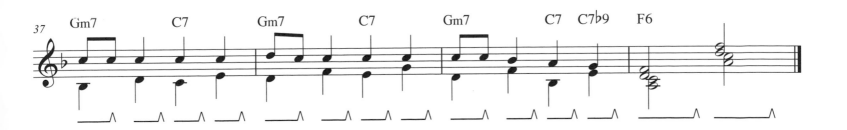

Have Yourself a Merry Little Christmas

Words and Music by Hugh Martin
and Ralph Blane

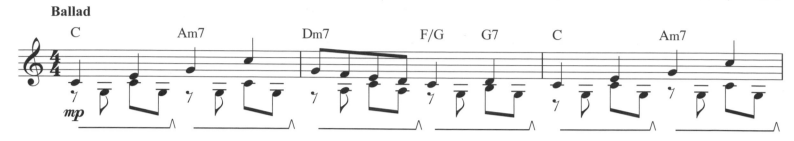

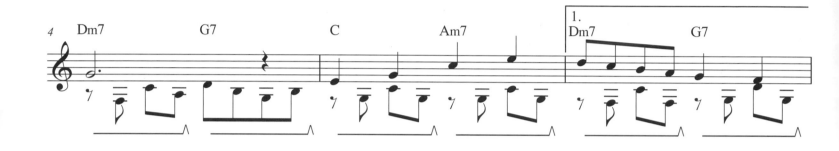

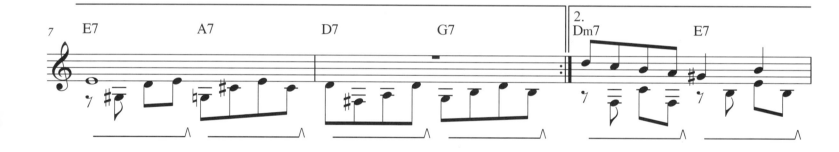

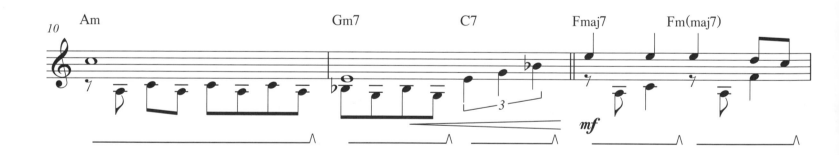

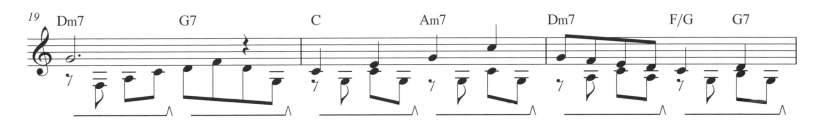

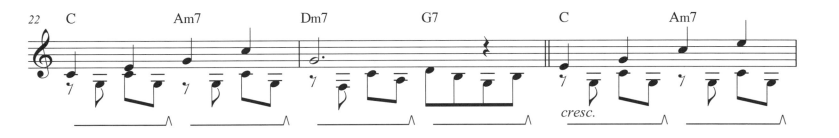

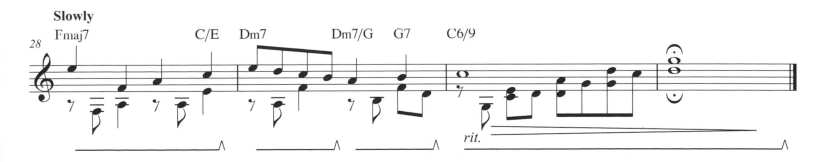

I'll Be Home for Christmas

Words and Music by Kim Gannon
and Walter Kent

× = Mallet dampen

Jingle Bell Rock

Words and Music by Joe Beal
and Jim Boothe

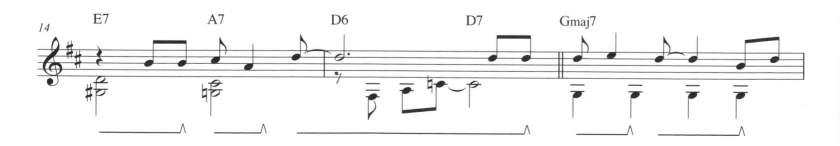

Rudolph the Red-Nosed Reindeer

× = Mallet dampen

Music and Lyrics by
Johnny Marks

Santa Baby

× = Mallet dampen

By Joan Javits,
Phil Springer and Tony Springer

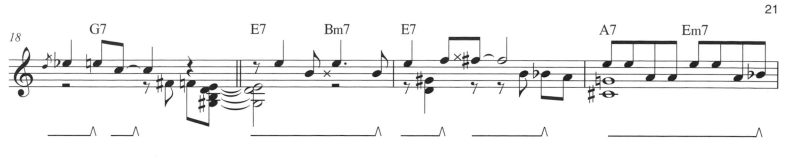

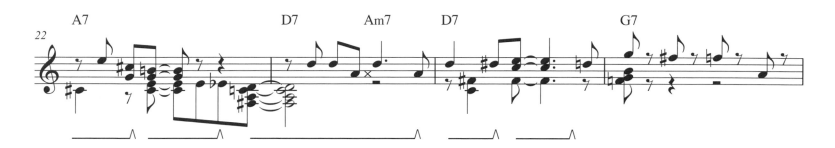

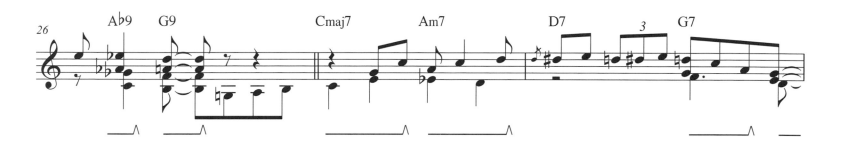

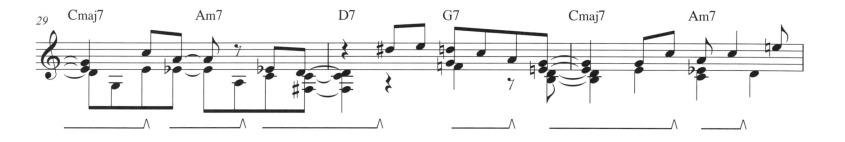

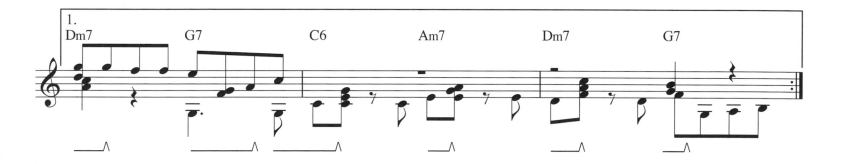

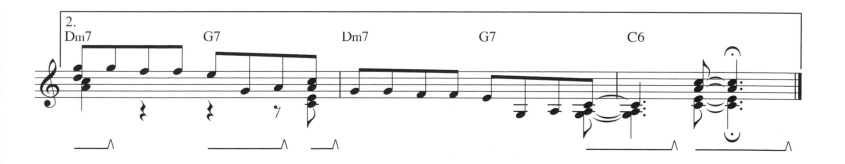

Silver Bells

Words and Music by Jay Livingston
and Ray Evans

× = Mallet dampen

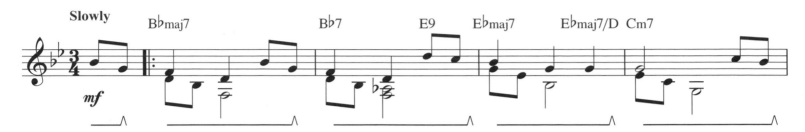

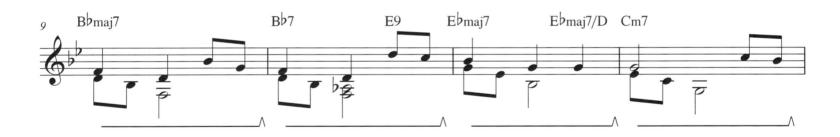

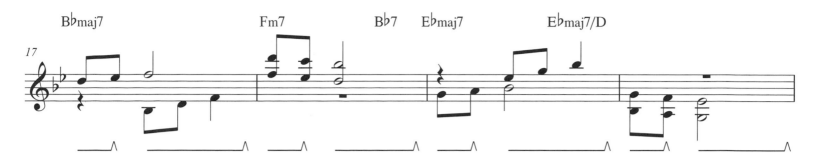

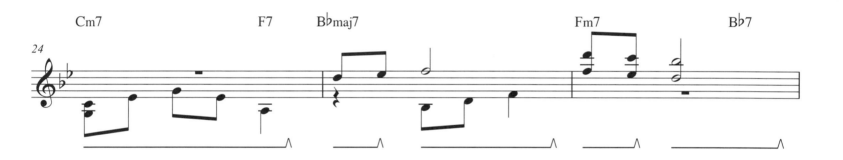

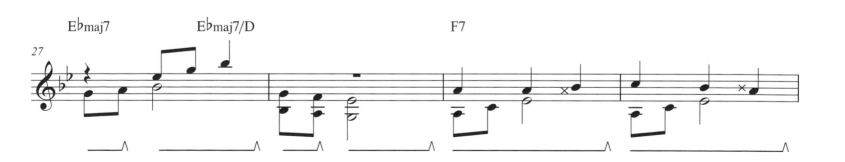

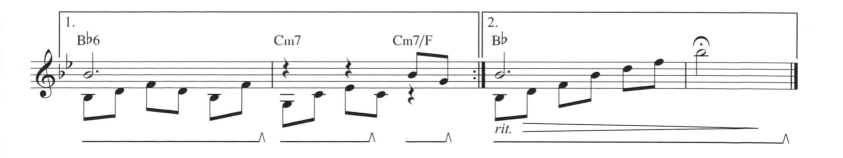

Sleigh Ride

Music by Leroy Anderson

White Christmas

Words and Music by
Irving Berlin

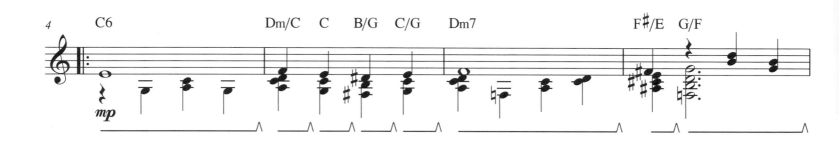

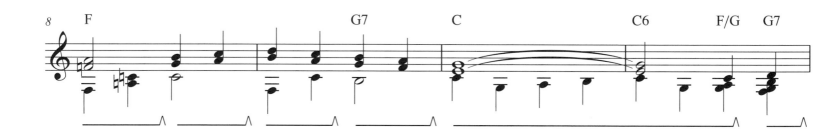

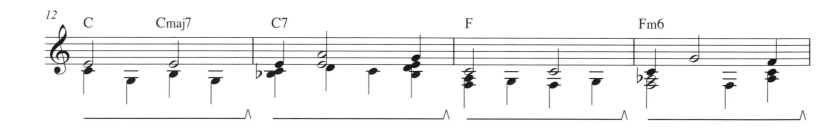

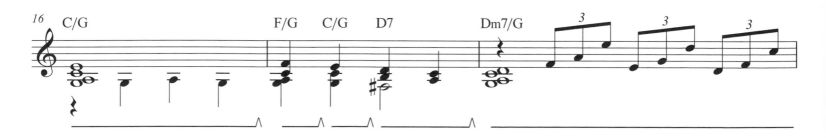

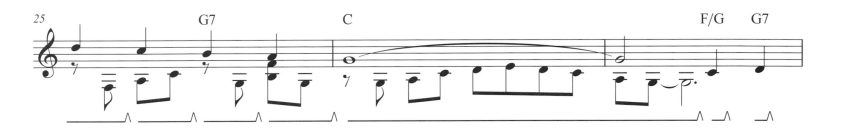

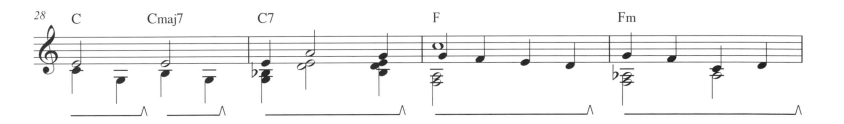

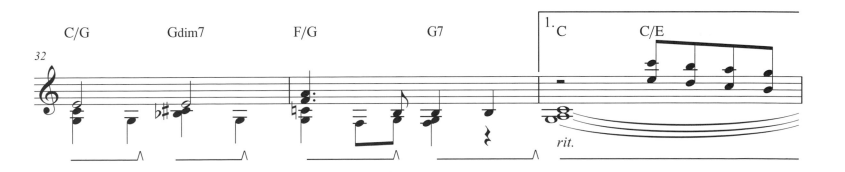

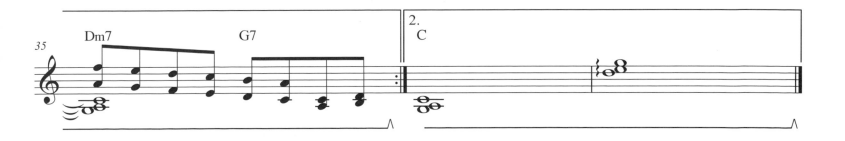

Winter Wonderland

Words by Dick Smith
Music by Felix Bernard

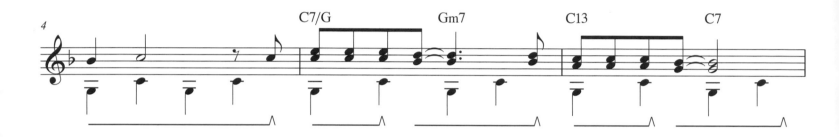

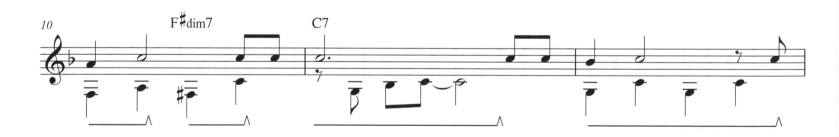

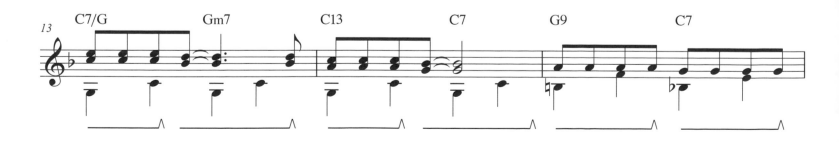

Here Comes Santa Claus
(Right Down Santa Claus Lane)

Words and Music by Gene Autry
and Oakley Haldeman

MASTER YOUR MALLET TECHNIQUE
with Hal Leonard

EXERCISES FOR MALLET INSTRUMENTS
Musical Etudes for Two and Four Mallets and Other Instruments
by Emil Richards

Exercises for Mallet Instruments contains jazz licks in all keys, adapted from the music of Debussy, Ravel, Bartok, Stravinsky, John Coltrane, and Charlie Parker. Practicing these etudes over jazz chords changes is an invaluable addition to the techniques of improvisation, and will improve reading skills. These 500 studies, along with seven original songs, were designed with the mallet player in mind, but will benefit any instrumentalist.
06620132 . . . .$19.99

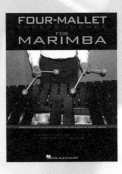

FOUR-MALLET INDEPENDENCE FOR MARIMBA
Progressive Studies for Two Mallets in Each Hand
by Johnny Lee Lane and Samuel A. Floyd, Jr.
edited by Richard L. Walker, Jr.

In this book, Johnny Lee Lane and Samuel A. Floyd, Jr. take you through a concentrated study of progressively arranged exercises. Through careful study and practice of the book's valuable musical examples, you will build a solid foundation in the independent manipulation of two mallets in each hand.
06620099 . . . .$9.95

FOUR-MALLET MARIMBA PLAYING
A Musical Approach for All Levels
by Nancy Zeltsman

This book contains a variety of music, from musical etudes designed for beginning and intermediate players, to recital material appropriate for intermediate and advanced marimbists. It includes: examples taken from contemporary solo and chamber works; 50 studies to develop four-mallet technique in a musical way; 18 classic and contemporary solos for recitals, auditions or juries; and helpful guidelines for mallet selection, grip, strokes, tone production, rolls, stickings, phrasing and other important topics.
06620055 . . . .$19.95

INTERMEDIATE PROGRESSIVE ETUDES
by David Kovins
The Vibraphone Virtuosity Series

This book/CD pack will help develop a contemporary vibist's technique and musicianship. It includes: 33 etudes in different styles; chromatic exercises; whole-tone scales; and studies in perfect fourths. It covers techniques such as: mallet dampening, pedaling, musical phrasing, and more. Each etude is performed on the accompanying disc, and some contain chord symbols to allow for improvisation.
06620026   Book/CD Pack $14.95

MALLET CHORD STUDIES
Chord Voicings and Arpeggio Patterns for Two and Four Mallets and Other Instruments
by Emil Richards

Mallet Chord Studies provides exercises that cover the open and closed positions found in most jazz phrasings on keyboard instruments. The etudes are designed to improve the improvisational skills needed to play all seventh chords in various open and closed positions. They will help the player to become proficient in moving from one chord and scale sequence to another. Though written primarily with mallet instrumentalists in mind, this practical book is suitable for any keyboard player.
06620134 . . . .$9.99

MELODY & RHYTHM PERMUTATIONS
More Than 300 Exercises for Mallets and Other Instruments
by Emil Richards

The exercises in *Melody & Rhythm Permutations* were developed to improve sight reading and improvisational skills in the advanced player. The inversions of melody and rhythm will keep the instrumentalist busy analyzing and performing these musical studies over the long haul, and a note from the author offers insights and practice suggestions. Though written primarily for mallet players, any instrumentalist will benefit from mastering these etudes.
06620135 . . . .$19.99

MODERN SCHOOL FOR MALLET-KEYBOARD INSTRUMENTS
by Jim Sewrey, Ben Hans and Tom Schneller
Edited by Rick Mattingly

This method features exercises and studies that cover the problems of technique in playing these instruments. Includes 30 progressive etudes, arrangements of violin concertos by Bach and Paganini for 'fixed-pitch' percussion, and orchestral excerpts from Ravel, Stravinsky, Shostakovich, Kabalevsky, Gershwin, Delibes, and others.
00347776 . . . .$14.99

SIGHT READING FOR MALLETS
by Emil Richards

As a long-time studio musician, Emil Richards knows the importance of sight reading and in this book has provided a superb source for those who would like to improve the skills needed to play today's music. *Sight Reading for Mallets* contains over 30 compositions that offer experience playing the unusual rhythms and phrases found in 21st-century writing. Though written primarily for mallets, any instrumentalist will gain the same benefits.
06620133 . . . .$12.99

VOICING AND COMPING FOR JAZZ VIBRAPHONE
by Thomas L. Davis

Here is the definitive guide to chordal playing for the contemporary vibraphonist. Includes material on: voicing selection, chord-member selection, use of extensions and alterations, voice leading, inversion selection, and more. The accompanying CD contains demos and play-along tracks with notated charts featuring standard chordal progressions in the following styles: fast & medium swing, ballad, jazz waltz, bossa-nova, and samba. This book is the most complete – and fun! – way to learn four-mallet voicings and comping patterns for jazz vibes.
06620019 Book/CD Pack $12.95

For more information, see your local music dealer, or write to:

HAL•LEONARD® CORPORATION
7777 W. BLUEMOUND RD. P.O. BOX 13819 MILWAUKEE, WI 53213

www.halleonard.com

Prices, contents, and availability subject to change without notice.

0612